Eldritch Raven /
Silly Goose

Jeramy De Luna

BookLeaf Publishing

India | USA | UK

Presentation by *BookLeaf Publishing*

Web: www.bookleafpub.com

E-mail: info@bookleafpub.com

ISBN: 9789363302020

First edition 2024

*To the drove of silly geese out there. To those
who love and put up with me.*

PREFACE

This is a collection of poems from my Write Angle writing challenge for BookLeaf Publishing.

Eldritch Raven / Silly Goose

You know the idea.
There are two dogs, wolves, etc. inside me.
Well, I see my internal duality set as more avian.
An Eldritch Raven and a Silly Goose.

An ebb and flow of grim understandings and
utter buffoonery.
A war with constant worst-case scenarios and
with randomly making loud Honks.
A struggle between the catastrophic and the
whimsical.

And this is where we find ourselves now.
In the in-between of the horror of the dark
recesses of the mind and the wild abandon of
humor.

I am here, in this clash and climax.
Ha... climax.

Lost adrift on a small vessel on the raging waves
of the sea in a storm.
But that ship is called the S.S. illy Goose.

The throws of whiplash back and forth between
these odd ends,
enough to break the minds of those who dare
venture into the brink,
is the only home my mind has ever known.

Also, oddly enough, may be the only place I do
feel at peace.
If I already played 24 outlandish and horrific
ways an interaction can go in my head, then I am
always prepared for the unexpected.

There might be some insight there.
Maybe the Raven is wise enough to know,
But the Goose is wearing a hat and jumping
around now...

Um.
Right.
Deep poem stuff goes here.

The Raven brings omens.
The Goose follows breadcrumbs.
Both are in flight now.

Silly Goose Haiku (a Honku, if you will)

a Honk outside
Silly Goose on loose
You are the Goose

A Bard's Lament

To be a bard is to sing songs of heroes and great
folk.
To have charisma, flair and the occasional dick
joke.

While always regaling others with these stories
and song,
They must constantly await a captive audience
to come along.

So when they wait, with eager melody for the
potential throngs,
The music is silent, and the thoughts come in
before too long.

If there are no others, then the bard must wait
idly by.
Just alone with thoughts and no outlet.
The muse tugging at their hearts, yet they cannot
part with their art.
To let it waste away on the wind, with no one to
listen.
No one to enjoy the rhythm or rhyme.
There is no greater despair.

They contemplate too much, question their
being.
A song sung by a choir of one is... lonely.

But what is that there?
A tavern, a pub, a fair?
A new audience.
To the bard's tunes, virgin ears, sweet credence.
Be gone existentialism.
Let us have distraction, merriment, and show off
witticism!

Enamored (sung to the tune of a B-52's song)

Come on girl, Let's play Twister!
Come on, Let's jump on the bed!
Go and play the boombox loud,
So we can rock our heads!

I got a full tank of gas and no place to be,
Let's go Cruising, baby, just you and me!

Thrill Me, Kill Me
Blow My Mind
You got me Insane,
Unsane
Love is Blind

Love at first sight

Feeling just left my body,
As soon as I looked and she saw me.
I'll just talk to her.
A conversation never hurt.
We'll talk through our busy day,
And we'll fall in love every other way.

Blank Music Sheet

The lines are blank, so live life loud
to fill it with your own music notes!

Fallen Hearts

For all the fallen hearts.
Relationships that never start.

For all the broken hearts.
Those left in the dark.

For the heartbreaker.
Who holds out because they just aren't sure.

For all the failed hearts.
For the plain people who love like art.

For all who never had a chance.
For all who just want to dance.

For all the relationships that are just dumb.
For all who would last till kingdom come.

For all the things that fell apart,
This is for all the fallen hearts.

Vacation Dream

I was standing on a beach. I could see all the way down the coast. I could see the waves of the ocean washing on the shore. There were palm trees more inland. The bright green of their leaves shone lush and vibrant in the warm sun. I could hear them rustle in the light breeze. I could hear the waves, washing back and forth. I could almost smell the salt water that saturated the air. I sat down and picked up a handful of hot sand. It was clean, white, and felt almost like powder. I let it drop through my fingers and took the whole place in.

Crows

The crows hover over,
And gather all together.
Flying over the dead body rotting,
One by one, they start dropping.
To meet the dead's soul,
That wanders to and fro.
Great fear he shows.
Seeing the black birds, he gains steadiness.
Feels the sense of readiness.
Knowing he is going to the land of the dead,
He slowly bows his head.
The crows lift the soul away.
In this world, he no longer has to stay,
With all its anger and hate.
The crows carried out the last of fate.
No longer in pain, no need to scream,
Just sleep and dream the crow black dream.

Bees

Be kind.
Save the bees.

Gray

Gray is everywhere you look.
Gray has everything overtook.
Gray is on the sidewalks and street.
Deep in my eyes when we meet.
Gray is in the very fork and knife you eat with.
Gray is on the wind that makes one drift.
Drift away slowly from humanity.
Drift away slowly into insanity.
Gray is the color of vague.
Gray is in all I crave.
Gray is your and my name engraved,
Side by side in our matching graves.
Gray is in everything in every way,
Because it will all slowly fade to gray.

The Last Stand of the Barbarian

The echoes of cries and rushing fade across the walls of this cave.
I told the party to leave, not because I think I am brave.
But because they can go and survive.
And I simply can't stand the beast to remain alive.
So they can go back to reset and rest away from this new stage.
They should not be here, when I finally let out the real rage.
It burns through my entire body and now it can be released,
Here, in the lair of the beast.
I stand, so small compared to its leviathan form,
But ready to unleash the raging storm.
The great beast charges forward, wanting to make a meal out of a failed escapee.
But I smile, because I am not trapped with it; the beast is trapped with me!

Star Collapse

Cannot quite shake this feeling
That time alone, won't help the healing.
My mind quietly turns,
With each thought, its own burn.
No stopping the silent desires
That set my mind on fire.
I will just endure, until it is ash.
Go insane, with each sear and lash.
Cannot stop what is set in motion,
Let it all go, grand final explosion.

Eldritch Raven

What a creeping corvid,
Loving the dark and morbid.
The wings do not flap; they beat.
Sharp beak, pecks, rips, tears flesh and meat.
There are ink-black eyes that stare.
Yet the eyes are more than two, you start to
notice the nightmare.
The feathers are a slick skin,
They pulse and writhe from within.
This foul fowl is something beyond
comprehension.
This horror, of extra dimension, focuses on you,
full attention.

Reminder for when dealing with people:

We are all just doing what we can.
Don't let it get to you too much.
Hurt People hurt people.
Remember that when dealing with such.

Adrift

Lost when space is the place.
Floating out past the stars, adrift so far.
Feeling mad, sad, and just alone.
Distress signal firing; please bring me home.

The empty, the expanding, the void, the vast.
Is it in my mind or outer space?
Am I fleeing the dead hand of the past?
Or did I just want to wander away from this
place?

Midnight Heart

Thump-Thump
In the late hour, the rush begins

Thump-Thump
The midnight heart stirs and strengthens

Thump-Thump
There is reaching out to find the rest of itself

Thump-Thump
Sensations surge and then there it extends
oneself

Thump-Thump
Finding home and solace in a fit so perfect

Thump-Thump
Suddenly the parts interconnect

Thump-Thump
For moments, hours, time means nothing

Thump-Thump
For the connection now, is everything

Thump-Thump
The midnight heart, united and fulfilled

Thump-Thump
After the late hour, now stilled

Space Envoi

All is stardust and
The universe thinking about itself.
All will return to stardust.
This is a difficult place to end on.

So maybe this then,
To paraphrase the Curiosity Rover,
My battery is low, and it is getting dark...